Awaken

Also by Michelle Carter

Loving You – Discover Your True Inner Self

Awaken

Michelle Carter

Love & Light
PUBLISHING

Copyright © 2016 Michelle Carter

All rights reserved. No part of this book may be used or reproduced by any means, graphic, electronic, or mechanical, including photocopying, recording, taping or by any information storage retrieval system without the written permission of the author, except in the case of brief quotations embodied in critical articles and reviews.

Because of the dynamic nature of the Internet, any web addresses or links contained in this book may have changed since publication and may no longer be valid.

Published by Love & Light Publishing

Paperback ISBN: - 978-0-9935931-2-3
E- book ISBN: - 978-0-9935931-1-6

Dedication

Dedicated with Pure Love, Light & Peace
To all those desiring to 'Awaken their Souls' and bring more Pure Love, Light, Peace and Truth to Earth.

And especially to you,
For choosing to read this book,
To make a difference

Contents

Acknowledgments...i
Introduction..iii
How Can You Awaken? 1
Energy – The Invisible Kind!..........................7
Disconnecting from Fear 19
Global Magnets or Collective......................23
Law of Attraction 29
Releasing & Cleansing 37
The Dominant Energy.................................45
The System 51
Discerning the Truth...................................61
How to Discern..63
Soul Barriers & Blocks to Feeling 71
How We Have Been Conned.......................81
Don't Play the Game! 85
What Can I do to Make a Difference? 91

The Power of Free Choice	97
Disconnecting from Mind Control	101
How Can We All Make a Difference?	105
Energy Work	113
Moving Forwards	119

Acknowledgments

We all have certain break-through moments in our life where something drops into place, we are given new information, or we realize why something was never going to work.

One of my first awakening moments was learning of Dr. Masaru Emoto's work with water and 'Messages in Water'. His lifetime of work has enlightened so many people. For me seeing the crystals he photographed was such a 'Wow moment!' I mean we often don't believe something until we see it, and energy and emotions are invisible, so here I was 'seeing the energy' of these emotions. This was very powerful information for me, and something I have never forgotten. So I would like to give much thanks and gratitude to Dr. Masaru Emoto and his team, for all his amazing work. You can see more about his work and images of the photographs he took on his website: - http://www.masaru-emoto.net

Another amazing breakthrough moment for me was whilst reading 'Power vs Force' by Dr. David Hawkins. The information he shared made many pieces of information I had in my head fit together and make sense. His description of the differences between the two powers, good and evil really felt true. I have used his research for the 'Human Scale of

Consciousness' for much of my energy healing work. I would therefore like to acknowledge and thank Dr. Hawkins for all his work and research.

Introduction

What if we were to open our minds to the possibility that there is an infinite power greater than humans, and that we could learn about this power and use it to positively transform our lives and also the whole world?

When we open our minds to new possibilities then huge positive change can happen. If we want a different outcome then we need to do something different. If you keep doing the same things and keep having the same beliefs, then you are going to keep getting the same result, so why not just try something new that could give you the most amazing result ever!

I feel that if more people were to understand and believe in energy and the "Power of the Universe', then not only can they positively transform their own life, but together we can unite our intentions and use the 'Power of the Universe' and 'Law of Attraction' to really create Peace on Earth.

So many people feel helpless and feel that they can't make a difference. I have written 'Awaken' with the aim to really awaken as many people as possible, to know that they can make a difference to their own life and the world. You don't need any knowledge of energy, healing or anything else to read 'Awaken'. It has been written in an easy to understand way, like I am having a chat with you and telling you all you need to know in order to learn something amazing! All you do need is an open mind and a willingness to learn.

'Awaken' is about awakening to how easy it can be for us all to use our thoughts, intentions and energy to transform our lives into much happier ones, feeling inner peace and harmony and connection to our hearts and souls. From this place of inner harmony we can then create a world filled with Love, Light, kindness, compassion and caring for all. We can create a world where we use natural renewable energies to look after our world and all who live on it. Then we can nourish our planet, instead of destroying and polluting it.

This is not a fairytale or a dream, this is possible and 'Awaken' has been written to walk you through how possible this is.

The important questions are:

**Do you want a better life for you and the world?
Are you willing to do something different to help create it?**

Reading 'Awaken' can help create both inner peace, world peace, and harmony, so let's get started and learn how we can 'Awaken'!

How Can You Awaken?

How can you 'Awaken'?

Well, there is no simple 'one sentence' answer to this, so I will explain as we go. My advice is to just open your mind and enjoy the journey, as we explore our world and the energy that makes everything work. Reading this book is going to be an adventure into the world of energy and it is probably best that you do read this book from the beginning to the end in order, as each chapter follows on from the last one, and it might not make sense if you jump in at the middle!

Pure Love, Light & Peace

In asking how can you 'Awaken', I suppose we could go back a step and ask, 'why do we need to 'Awaken'?' The answer to this is because: -

We have lack, illness, war and discontentment across the globe and the majority of people on earth want to live in love, peace, happiness and abundance.

If the majority of people do not want war and all that goes with it, then isn't it up to us, the majority, to do something to stop us being at war, in lack and living in fear? The answer is of course a huge YES, but I know that so many people, and that used to include myself too, don't believe we can make a difference. We feel we are just one person with no power against governments and all those making the decisions, and no power over people with guns and bombs.

However, when we unite and use our majority intention together, we do have huge power and that is what 'Awaken' is all about: -

Using our group intention to create peace and inner harmony and happiness for all.

The good news is that anyone who chooses peace and harmony can add their energy to the group intention right now, in their own home with the information in this book!

Awaken

In fact, anyone can help create peace without even knowing any of the behind the scenes facts or discovering the Truth. What action appeals to you after reading this book is your choice and you need to follow your own feelings to do what is right for you. Every little thing we all do is adding to the collective intention to create peace and that can only be good! So let's get started . . . but where on earth do we start? Well, let's start with why I have written 'Awaken' and what I hope to achieve for you as you read it.

I have written 'Awaken' in a light-hearted and easy to read style, so that you enjoy reading all the information contained in these pages. Many readers of my previous book 'Loving You – Discover Your True Inner Self' commented on how much they liked the 'easy going style' of my writing, and that it felt like I was having a cozy chat with them! We are more willing to be open to new information if we feel happy and relaxed, so I have also infused 'Awaken' with powerful Pure and Divine Energies so that you feel peaceful and inspired as you read!

I have included energy work and releasing statements, like the one below, (which I will explain later in more detail), so just enjoy being open-minded, and have fun with the process of learning more as you read: -

"I choose to be open to new ideas and release any resistance to learning something new. I understand that learning about something new can be fun and

Pure Love, Light & Peace

exciting and has no threat to me, or my existing views, as I don't have to change anything I believe, unless I choose to change it. I feel safe and excited to learn new ideas and to be open to new possibilities!'

Finding out why we have disharmony when the majority of people want to live in peace and happiness is one way of moving towards peace. I mean how can we change something if we don't know what is wrong?

Well there are two aspects to life: -

- Our human life, knowledge and awareness
- 'The Power of the Universe', the universal life force behind of all life

In terms of human life and human systems, it is very true to say that we do need to know what is wrong before we can change the system to a better one.

However in terms of the whole universe there is a whole system of power all around us, that most of the Western World do not acknowledge exists, and certainly don't use it to their advantage.

What if we were to open our minds to the possibility that there is an infinite power greater than humans, and that we could learn about this power and use it to create peace on earth? Now wouldn't that be a really amazing thing to do? Of course it would! So let's start by opening our minds to . . . whatever!

Awaken

Let's leave religion and politics out, in fact we are going to leave all human systems and beliefs out and we are going to talk about energy . . . Universal Energy!

Pure Love, Light & Peace

Energy – The Invisible Kind!

We all know and accept that energy exists when we think of what makes our appliances and remote controls work.

Also we acknowledge and understand that there is natural energy, such as the sun, wind and water that can be converted into power for our human means. So a really simple, non-scientific explanation of 'what is energy', could be - it is the power that can be used to make something 'without its own source of power' work.

Pure Love, Light & Peace

We all believe in energy and know it exists because we use energy all day, everyday for our appliances, from home appliances and electronic appliances, running from the mains electricity or battery power and our vehicles using fuel as energy. Sometimes we can see the source of energy as in petrol or gas for our vehicles and sometimes we can't see it, as in electricity, where we plug into the mains, but don't see the electricity flow like we can if we pour fuel into a can.

There is also invisible energy such as WI-FI and satellite signals. We believe these exist because we can see the result on our phones, computers and TVs.

We can dig deeper and go more into energy and quantum physics, but don't worry I'm not a scientific person, so we're not going there! We do however need to know that energy can be measured and when we do measure it, there are lots of different types of energy.

If we take sound, we know we have high and low sounds and musical notes, and we can hear the difference between them. In terms of energy, the higher sounds move or vibrate quicker than the lower sounds. The higher sound has a higher frequency so it vibrates more quickly than lower sounds.

Like sound, all energy can be measured by how fast the particles vibrate. Fast vibrating energy has a high vibration or frequency, and slow vibrating energy has a low vibration or frequency. As humans we are tuned into seeing, hearing and sensing certain frequencies of energy, and usually we all agree on what we can and can't see. Having said that, some people can see energy and auras that most people cannot see, and this can be captured and seen by special photography called Kirlian photography. Also dogs and animals can hear a higher frequency of sound than humans. I've even heard that teenagers can hear a different range of sound to adults. This fact is used to deter teenagers from hanging out in certain places at night, by playing a certain frequency of sound that will sound awful, even painful to teenagers, whilst adults and younger children won't hear it. So we do need to acknowledge and realize that we are all different. What appears to be so for one person is not so for another, and this can and does change throughout our lives as we change with age, hormones and awareness!

Western beliefs tend to make fun of anything that we cannot see and make out that they don't exist, or that people who believe in them are crazy. However, this is just a belief that has been very well programmed into most westerners, which isn't true. If we had been brought up as a native living in nature, then we would have totally different beliefs, and would probably think that using computers and phones is ridiculous when you can connect through nature, intuition and telepath connections! It is important that we realize the difference between a belief and what is actually true.

Pure Love, Light & Peace

Truth is true for all people regardless of where they live and what beliefs they have been told.

It is true that we will all die and leave our physical bodies? Well it is at this point in time, but who knows if this will always be true? We assume it will be, but do we actually know this for sure? So we do need to question whether what we believe is actually true, or if it is a belief. Much of what we do believe, has been programmed into us, from birth, by society, and as I have already mentioned, if we had been born into a different society then we would have different beliefs, which shows that beliefs and truth are very different.

We have just touched on a very important point, so I would like to emphasize this point and chat about it a bit more.

*Beliefs are not Truth, they are beliefs,
Truth is true for everyone.*

Beliefs belong to a group of people. Each religion, culture, school, workplace, political party and so on all have their own beliefs that they teach to all those in their group. This teaching is done in such a way that we are meant to believe it is Truth, and this in fact causes so many issues relating to war and discrimination.

When we understand that if we had been born into a different family, in a different country, with a different religion and culture, then we would have different beliefs. So no set of beliefs is true, it is the opinions of that group of people. Another way of seeing this is language. If we take the word 'table', each country will have a word for 'table' and everyone in each country will understand that word means table. Across the world there will be many words for table and they are all correct for each language. However, the English word for table isn't Truth, whilst the French word is wrong, they are all different versions of the same thing, and we don't fight about which is the correct version or word for table, we understand that we all have our own language. The same is true for our beliefs, we all have different beliefs and none are more correct than the others, they are all just different versions of the same thing.

Truth on the other hand is true for the whole of the world. Truth does not change with opinion, just like our 'Universal Laws', they don't change for each country, religion or group of people, they are true for all. The 'Law of Gravity' applies to all people, animals and objects on earth, and no belief or even hypnosis can overwrite this. The same is true for the 'Law of Attraction' and other universal laws; they are true for all energy and cannot be changed by any human means. When we are in tune with the universe and source energy then we can feel what is Truth and what is not.

Pure Love, Light & Peace

I seem to have digressed from energy to Truth, so let's go back to energy. We need to know that all energy comes from a source and that this source is either pure or evil.

Some people don't like to believe that evil and dark exists because it brings up fear in them, and I totally understand this as I have been there. However, when we look at the state of the world with war, rape, abuse, lack, poverty, disease and so on, then it seems pretty obvious that evil does exist. To say that evil and dark don't exist is saying that all these horrendous actions come from one source. Well to me that is a pretty scary thought. If there is only one source in control, then how do we know if this source is going to kick out good things or bad things? It's a bit like the world source is being controlled by hormones and the female cycle; when the hormones are calm we get a kind, caring, loving world, but when the hormones are triggered, look out because all hell breaks loose and who knows what will happen, so stay well clear! (Being female and having lived through how female hormones can suddenly erupt out of nowhere, I know how random this can be.) Fortunately this is not how the universe works!

Can good and bad actions come from the same source?

Well to answer this we need to know more about how different energies can be measured.

Awaken

My first experiences of energy being measured, was from reading one of Dr. Masaru Emoto's books, on 'The Messages in Water'. In summary, he exposed water to different energies, froze the water and then photographed the water crystals. What he discovered was, that when he exposed water to positive words such as 'love', 'gratitude', Truth, 'eternal', and 'thank you', beautiful crystals were formed. When the water was exposed to negative words such as 'hate', 'evil' and 'you fool', broken and incomplete crystals were formed.

He also worked with different styles of music, animals, plants, flower essences, speeches, prayers, and the crystals followed the same pattern. All pure energies gave beautifully formed crystals and non-pure energies gave broken crystals.

This shows that there is a difference between good and bad, pure and evil, and this difference can be SEEN in water crystals. (You can check out his work and see these photographs on his website: -
www.masaru-emoto.net)

These photographs show that our invisible energy is not so invisible! We can't see emotions with our human eyes, but we all feel emotions and we know they exist, and looking at the crystal photographs shows us what these invisible emotions look like. The water was the same until it was exposed to different energies, which then altered the water so much that it

Pure Love, Light & Peace

looks completely different when frozen and seen under a microscope.

Since our physical bodies are over 60% water, then consider the effect that energy around us has on our bodies and health – pollution, food, drinks, emotions, etc. will all be impacting the water inside our cells all the time and altering them. That really opens our eyes to how easy it is to become ill and depressed. All the energies surrounding us will be affecting the water in our cells, and changing them, so if we spend lots of time surrounded by negative, destructive, low vibrating energies then this will have a negative impact on our health through the water in our cells.

We can see from Dr. Emoto's work that we have two main energies on earth, pure and evil, that affect water in different ways. Pure and evil are opposite energies, and they conflict each other. Pure consists of everything that makes us feel good, uplifted, supported and loved, so unconditional love, joy, happiness, kindness, caring, compassion, and sharing are all pure energies. Evil consists of everything that makes us feel bad, used, taken advantage of, so abuse, lies, manipulation, hate, control, slavery, war, and killing are all evil energies.

Pure energy is natural and it exists without us having to do anything, like the sun, light, water, wind, rivers, seas and oceans. Humans don't create these energies, they are a part of nature and naturally exist. Evil energy doesn't exist naturally, it is created by human means, through evil desires, to control other humans through any means.

In his book, 'Power vs Force', Dr. David Hawkins talks about the difference between pure and evil in terms of power vs force and natural vs manmade. Here is what he says about the differences between power and force: -

"Force is incomplete and therefore has to be fed energy constantly. Power is total and complete in itself and requires nothing from outside.
It makes no demands, it has no needs.

Because force has an insatiable appetite, it constantly consumes. Power in contrast, energizes, gives forth, supplies, and supports. Power gives life and energy – force takes these away. We notice that power is associated with compassion and makes us feel positively about ourselves. Force is associated with judgment and makes us feel poorly about ourselves."

Well let's break this down and talk about it in more detail because this is such enlightening information, like really enlightening! In fact, the first two sentences really sums up Light and dark or Pure and evil: -

"Power is total and complete in itself and requires nothing from outside. It makes no demands, it has no needs."

Pure Love, Light & Peace

The sun is pure energy, it is natural power, it shines regardless of what we do as humans, it shines regardless of the clouds in the sky, it is still shining behind the clouds, and it shines day and night; we only see it during our daytime because it is shining in the opposite hemisphere during our night, as the earth rotates. The sun makes no demands of humans and has no needs from us.

Pure energy is the highest frequency energy there is and it can only be Pure. It does not suddenly lower its vibration, act like dark and evil energy and then return to being Pure again! Pure energy remains pure energy regardless of what is happening around it.

"Force is incomplete and therefore has to be fed energy constantly. Force has an insatiable appetite, it constantly consumes"

Evil has no natural source of energy and needs to be fed energy constantly. Evil and dark need to create their own energy; without it they have no power. They make their energy by creating fear, shock, upset, grief and other low emotions. Anything that is a low vibration is the opposite of pure energy and it is fuel that feeds evil.

This information is actually very EMPOWERING! To know that 'Pure Energy' exists naturally without us doing anything is hugely comforting information. All the pure energy we desire just exists, regardless of what we do, think or believe. Now that's probably just as well, don't you think! Then added to that we now know that evil has to create ALL its energy from scratch. It is also enlightening to know this, because if evil cannot create its own energy then it cannot exist.

Evil is not a natural energy and needs to create energy to exist. If evil cannot create it's own energy, then it cannot exist.

It would make sense then, knowing this, that to stop evil existing all we need to do is to find a way to stop it being able to create its own energy. So if everyone in the world felt peace and stillness for just one second, then in that one second no evil could be created. Obviously, just saying to people don't feel fear, sadness, trauma or grief isn't going to work, because we all know that feelings are very powerful and they kind of take over us when we are feeling them. However, when we have the awareness that all low emotions are feeding evil, we can then be far more supportive of ourselves and others to move out of these feelings as quickly as possible. This means that not only can we feel better quicker, but also we are not creating energy for evil means.

Awareness is a very powerful tool; when enough people are aware of the negative power in all low emotions then we can all work together to stop evil

Pure Love, Light & Peace

creating its own energy. When evil cannot create its own energy it will no longer exist on earth.

Whilst it is not easy for us to just choose to not be angry, upset, in fear and so on, it is actually a fairly easy process for us to use energy healing to disconnect from feeling these emotions, which means that we will no longer feel them. I have done this disconnecting work on others, and myself with amazing results, mainly that when we would have expected to feel fear, trauma or upset we have felt calm instead. Now this is powerful stuff! Imagine if half the population of the world were to disconnect from all these low emotions, and didn't create any dark energy for evil to use against us . . . the world would certainly be a much happier, brighter, and more peaceful place to live!

Now this is the reason I have written this book – to show you how we can disconnect from fear and all negative energies, so we can stop living in fear, lack, illness, disharmony, etc. which feeds the evil that creates war.

When there is no fear or negative energy in the world there will be no evil, dark or war, because there will be no energy to feed and create wars and evil behavior.

So now would be a good time to learn about how we can disconnect from fear, and it's really easy, you just need to keep reading!

Disconnecting from Fear

Before we can fully understand how to disconnect from fear, we do need to discuss energy in more detail, along with the Law of Attraction, but for now, let's read some 'Disconnecting Statements' and just walk through the process and see how we feel. We will go into the details about it later.

Notice what you feel as you read these statements: -

"I disconnect from fear now"

"Pure Love & Light disconnects me from fear now"

Pure Love, Light & Peace

"Pure Source Energy / The Power of the Universe disconnects me from fear now"

When I read these statements I can feel more energy shifting in each statement, i.e. each statement feels more powerful than the last one. This is because the first statement is just using my energy, (or yours when you read it) and the other statements are using more powerful 'universal energies'. From what we feel, we can tell that universal energy is more powerful than our own personal energy and this what we would expect.

If you don't feel anything then please don't worry, it can take a while for some people to open up to feeling the energy. If you keep reading these statements, and those at the back of this book, you will start to feel energy as it 'shifts', which means it is leaving us and going. Determination and effort will reap good rewards here, so just keep doing it until you feel something, then you will be so excited!

Pure Love & Light / Pure Source Energy / the Power of the Universe are all different ways of describing the 'Pure Energy' that naturally exists. Different people prefer different names to express this energy and that is ok. There are many countries in the world and many different languages, so there are many different words for every word that exists, such as table, world, apple, food, love etc. and we all accept this is so. Even if we are all using English we can still have different words in different countries for the same word, for example, in England we have 'rubbish' or 'waste', while in America it is 'trash' or 'garbage'. We may find this amusing, especially when we add in the different accents! Not many people are hugely upset over this, and we just accept we have different names and accents. So please choose whatever phrase you like, and I will use whichever seems right to me at the time!

When we use Pure Source Energy it has more power than using our own energy because, well, the universe and source energy is a very high frequency and very powerful!

We can start to disconnect from fear just by reading or saying the statement below. The more intention, emotion or feeling we connect to the statement as we read it, then the more powerful the result will be. You can experiment with this yourself and notice what you feel.

"Pure Source Energy / The Power of the Universe Disconnects me from fear now"

You can be more specific and add extra words to this statement, such as 'fear of war', 'fear of being attacked', 'fear of dark', 'fear of evil' and so on. The more specific we are, the easier and quicker it is to disconnect. If we are very specific, it's a bit like pulling out one weed from the root and getting the whole root out, whereas if we are more general, it's more like trying to pull out lots of roots all at once, where they break off and half the root stays in the ground and we just take the surface leaves off.

If you prefer to have energy work done for you, then I have recorded 'Disconnecting from Fear' as an audio so you can just listen and know that powerful energy work is being done for you. (Details on my website, www.michellecarter.co.uk)

To understand this more we need to discuss global magnets in relation to personal magnets and collective consciousness.

Awaken

Global Magnets or Collective Consciousness

We all have our own 'personal magnets' or 'energy field' that consists of everything that we have connected with during our life, all emotions, beliefs, people, places, experiences etc. So it is a bit like our whole life is being stored in magnetic form around us.

Global magnets store all the world's energy from the beginning of its creation; all of the beliefs, emotions, issues and experiences that have ever happened - wow, now isn't that a lot of energy! Much of the global energy is not pure and positive. Do we really want to be connected to all of the wars, murders, rape, abuse, lack, poverty, illness and disease that have ever existed? I'd say not, in fact, it's a huge NO!

The thing is, we **are** connected to this global energy, even if we aren't aware of it, and these 'global magnets' or 'collective consciousness' are affecting us and our lives every second of every day! How it affects us will depend on our personal magnets or energy field. We are all unique people with very different lives, experiences and past lives, so the energy that we have collected and stored within us will differ from person to person.

If you continue to do a certain thing or attract an unwanted behavior or person into your life, this is because you have these negative energies stored in you, which are interacting with the collective consciousness and the global magnets of the whole world throughout each day.

Let's discuss this some more and explain it further, and then I will give you a visual example which I hope will help you to fully understand the magnetic power and pull of energy and how it is affecting us all the time.

Everything in the world is a type of energy, from emotions and beliefs, to rooms and furniture, to towns, religions, groups and individual people. They are all made of energy. People have many different frequencies of energy inside of them. We are all filled with stored emotions, beliefs, memories, illnesses and accidents. Literally everything that has ever happened to us in our life is stored in us as energy.

All energy has a magnetic affect and is either coming from a Pure energy source or a dark energy source.

Our energy is bigger than just our physical body, we actually have energy stored in our mind as all our thoughts, heart as all our emotions, soul as Divine integrity and moral values, physical body, aura and all past lives. We can call this collection of energy our 'energy being' and can imagine it as a big bubble that surrounds us. Then we can imagine that each emotion, belief, memory, illness, etc. is a leaf floating around inside of our 'energy being', each having a magnetic affect on us, from either a Pure energy or a dark energy source.

Then we have the rest of the world, which is like a huge forest of leaves, again some Pure energy and some dark energy, and all the energies that exist in between Pure and evil. Living is like going for a walk in the forest, with all these leaves swirling around us, and the type of leaves we walk through depends on which way we walk. We know that some of the leaves floating around us are dark and not good for us, and we know that some are Pure and will make us happy and improve our lives, but how do we know which are which?

Pure Love, Light & Peace

If the colour of the leaf showed us what type of energy it was, then it would be easy for us to see which leaves we wanted to connect with, and which ones we wanted to avoid, i.e. if leaves from a dark source were dark coloured, black, brown and dark grey, we would know to stay away from these leaves, whilst leaves from a Pure source were pastel colours and white, then we would know that these leaves were Pure and good for us.

This will make walking around the forest and knowing which path to choose so much easier! However we can't see energy, or at least most people can't, so we need another way to know which energy is going to improve our lives, and which is a disaster area to avoid. We can do this though our feelings and this is called feeling intuitive; it is our feelings guiding us as to what in our lives is good energy and what is not.

As I've said before, in western society we are not encouraged to tune into and use our intuition, in fact we are made to feel we are crazy if we talk about it and do it! When you really understand energy and how it works it becomes crazy to not tune into and follow your intuition!

Instead of using colours for our leaves we can use another visual example of having a black and white scale. If you prefer numbers, you can have a numerical scale of -1000 to 1000, however the number isn't the important part. Imagine all the shades of grey that exist between black and white, or all the numbers, decimals and fractions that exist between -1000 and 1000. Quite a few! This gives us a visual example of how many variations of energy exist between Pure and evil.

Every person and everything on earth has a range on these visual scales, between Pure and evil. We will yo-yo between our highest and lowest points of our range on the scale, and our range can slide up and down the scale too.

So we are walking through the forest of life and we can see or feel all the different energies around us, so we know that there are some we don't want to connect with and some we do. This makes life really easy now, right? Well it is certainly easier with this knowledge, but remember that all the leaves or energies are magnetic and we are magnetic, so the magnetic force between our magnets and global magnets can be triggered without us wanting them to be triggered. For example, as we are walking about in the forest, we might stumble across some negative energies, (anything that would upset us in any way, such as an unexpected upsetting phone call), that triggers some magnets in us, so we now feel upset, sad, or angry even though we were fine before we stumbled onto these energies. To understand how this happens we need to talk about the Law of Attraction and how this affects us.

Pure Love, Light & Peace

I'm sure you have had experiences in your life where you ended up in a bad place, situation or experience without wanting to, or without intentionally choosing that to happen. Just being aware of this isn't enough, as there is more going on behind the scenes.

Awaken

Law of Attraction

We have all heard of the Law of Attraction, but do we fully understand it?

It states: -

"Like Attracts Like, and Opposites Repel"

Pure attracts Pure, evil attracts evil and Pure repels evil. So fun, love, laughter attracts more of these emotions, and hate, fear, violence also attract more of the same, whilst love repels fear and violence and so on.

Pure Love, Light & Peace

If we are amongst many grieving people, as we would be at a funeral, then any stored 'grief magnets' in our energy field will be activated and we feel grief. The more grief magnets we have inside us, the more intense we will feel the grief. Also the more grief magnets there are in the whole group at the funeral, the more this will affect us too.

We all have our own magnetic energy, which can be triggered by the global energy magnets around us. How much the energy around us affects and triggers us depends on how strong that energy is, i.e. one person being upset and crying will have a less powerful effect on us than 20 people all being upset and crying, because with more people the energy is intensified and the magnetic affect is also more intensified. It also depends on how many of those magnets we have stored in us and how close to the surface they are. If we don't have too many upset emotions stored, then we may not be triggered. However, if we have just been through a very upsetting life experience, then we will have many upset emotions on the surface, which will trigger us to feel and express this upset quicker than if the incident was more in our past. We will also react more easily than someone with fewer upset emotions stored. (We will discuss this more in the chapter 'Releasing and Clearing'.)

This is why major traumatic global events can affect us so much, because there are so many people being affected and triggered that the total global magnetic affect is huge, and this has a deep magnetic affect on us, especially if we are very empathic and caring.

The energy magnets we are exposed to from conception onwards will have a profound affect on us. For example, if someone is born into a family where they felt unloved, or they didn't have a family at all, then they will feel unloved, and will start to collect magnets of 'feeling unloved', and similar magnets such as 'not wanted', 'not good enough' and even 'abandoned'. As their life progresses they will collect more and more of these magnets unless their life dramatically changes and they start to feel loved, and then they can start to collect magnets of 'love', 'being loved', 'wanted', 'good enough' and 'cherished'.

Our early experiences of life are so important because these will give us our first or main magnets. These magnets will be hard at work behind the scenes, collecting more 'like magnets' and all this is occurring before we are old enough to be aware of what is happening to us. So our life is very much shaped around our early experiences, if we collect positive magnets in our early years, life will be easier, however if we are collecting negative magnets, then this makes life far more challenging and can create destructive patterns that are hard to break, such as addictions, self-abuse, lack of confidence and belief in yourself.

Whatever we experience throughout our life is stored within us, and will attract more of the same to us. So

Pure Love, Light & Peace

as I've said above, this is great if we have been born into a loving, caring family and have been showered with love and felt abundance; not so good if we haven't. This is where energy comes in, where we can do daily energy work to release and get rid of those magnets that are not serving us, so they are not attracting bad experiences to us and making our lives hell to live.

Every thought, belief, feeling, emotion, program or pattern is stored inside us and these energy magnets can be activated and triggered by 'like magnets' around us as we connect with other people and things.

We know that if we enter a room where people are or have been arguing, we can feel the energy and it makes us feel uncomfortable and not want to be there. Likewise if we enter a room full of people laughing, having fun and celebrating, then we feel the joy and excitement and want to be a part of it, or feel uplifted as we continue our day.

The most dominant magnets in us are the ones that are most likely to be triggered, just because there are more of them. If your energy field is full of magnets of depression and feeling low, alone and down then you will be attracted to similar magnets, which is what makes it so hard to shift out of depression when we are attracting 'like magnets'.

Awaken

Sometimes the magnets are hidden and shut away so we don't feel the pain. We subconsciously shut the emotional pain away and don't think about it or feel it. This can work for us short term, but is a bit like sitting on a time bomb, as eventually the hidden magnets will be triggered by a powerful group or global magnet outside of us. This will cause a sudden, massive reaction, out burst of temper, anger or an unexpected emotional outburst out of nowhere, or even further down the line a nervous breakdown. The reaction will depend on the type of energy magnet that has been triggered.

When we are aware of energy magnets and what is happening to us, we have 'Free Choice' so we can choose to get rid of or release the negative stored magnets in us so they can't randomly erupt on us!

Not only can we release emotions we don't want, but we can also release beliefs, thoughts, patterns, programming, illnesses, or anything else that we don't want influencing our lives.

Releasing unwanted energies has been a huge part of my Divine Energy work, along with channeling Pure Divine Energies, to 'kick out' the impure energies, and then fill the space with Pure energies, so the unwanted ones can't sneak back in!

In principle, releasing is very easy to do. In practice, the effectiveness of it depends on your ability to

Pure Love, Light & Peace

connect to and channel Pure Divine Energy, to 'out power' the lower vibrations of energy and release them. I discovered the more I worked on myself, the more powerful my channeling became; and as my energy and channel became clearer, it allowed more Pure energy to flow, making it easier to do powerful work on others.

For a visual example, imagine a blocked drain where the water starts to go down the drain really slowly, if the block isn't cleared and gets worse the water will flow less and less, until eventually it becomes so blocked that the water stops flowing altogether and overflows around the drain area. As we start to remove the blockage, the water starts to run slowly down the drain again. When the blockage is completely removed the water will easily flow down the drain.

Our energy is the same, if we clear it and keep it clear then we are not storing unwanted magnets. If we don't keep clearing our energy then we are constantly collecting and storing more unwanted magnets until we have a physical or mental crash in our lives, (ill health, financial issues, relationship break up, etc.) When this happens most people will look at their life in a different way, which is often when people discover spirituality and awaken to energy healing and the power of energy.

Awaken

Having learnt about how our energy is collecting unwanted magnets and creating blocks, I am assuming that you'd like to learn how to unblock your blocks! We call this 'Releasing and Cleansing' our energy. So let's find out how we do this!

Pure Love, Light & Peace

Awaken

Releasing & Cleansing

Releasing is the term we use to get rid of blocks in our energy, like the block in the drain that is stopping the flow of water. Whenever our life feels stuck or not happy and not flowing then there will be something that needs to be released through energy.

Cleansing is more of an on-going daily routine that we do to keep our energy clean, a bit like taking a daily shower and cleaning our teeth morning and night.

To be able to powerfully release blocked energies we need to have a clear channel. To have a clear channel

Pure Love, Light & Peace

we need to have released our stored unwanted magnets . . . so this can be a bit of a catch 22 situation!

As Einstein said: -

"You cannot solve a problem from the same level of consciousness that created it"

I.e. we need a 'higher power energy' to shift a block or issue than the issue itself.

So if you are feeling low and depressed, then you need a higher energy than the feelings of low and depressed, to lift yourself out of these feelings and out of this energy. If the low feeling is temporary, say due to a bad day or a small upset, then it is fairly easy to use higher energies to raise our vibration and feel better.

Energies we can use to raise our vibration include: -

- Fun, lively music or video clips
- Looking at happy photos and memories
- Reminding yourself of fun times you've had and feeling the happiness
- Chatting to upbeat, happy friends
- Smelling essential oils that raise our vibration, I love rose oil!
- Spending time outside in nature, breathing fresh air

Awaken

- Walking on a beach or in wood or park can help the low mood to shift out
- Indoor exercise, especially to music you love will motivate you and bring in some feel good factor!
- Eating dark chocolate! Yes it's full of magnesium which has the 'feel good' hormones in it, and dark chocolate is low in sugar so no need to feel guilty either!

If the depressed energy is deeper and has been there long term, caused by abuse, addictions, long term depression, feeling suicidal, unworthy, unloved, useless, or grief that isn't healed, then these are all very damaging energies that eat away at us if we don't get out of these feelings and energy. This is when the higher, more powerful energy is needed and where 'Energy Healing and Releasing' really can change lives.

As a Divine Energy Channel, I call in The Power of the Universe, Pure Source Energy or Divine Energies to release destructive, negative and dark energies from people, places and issues. I ask for the negative and dark energies to be sent to Pure Source to be purified, and fill the space with more Pure energies, usually Pure Love & Light.

A Releasing Statement can be as simple as: -

"I release all energies of sadness from me now."

Pure Love, Light & Peace

Or

"I ask Pure Love and Light to release all energies causing and creating sadness in me now."

"I ask Pure Source Energy / The Power of the Universe to release all energies causing and creating sadness in me now."

Or the complete statement will be: -

"I ask Pure Source Energy / The Power of the Universe to release all energies causing and creating sadness in me now, to send all these energies direct to source to be purified and fill with Pure Love & Light."

You can change 'sadness' for any emotion or belief you wish to let go of right now. When you can feel energy, you will feel that the last two statements feel better than the first and the complete statement is the most powerful.

The vibration of Pure Love and Light is very high and totally Pure, so it has the ability to shift all energies from within us, only being restricted if there are blocks stopping it from working.

This may lead you to ask, 'What can block Pure Love and Light?' which is a very good question! Which brings us back to the two opposite energies of Pure and evil, or Light and dark.

Awaken

Light is more powerful than dark.

If we turn on a light in a dark room the whole room lights up, not just the bit around the light. When there are no clouds in the sky, the sun lights up and warms up everything below it.

So if Light is more powerful than dark, then how can anything block Light?

If we imagine that Pure Source Light is the sun, on a sunny day the sun shines and we can all see the sun up in a blue sky and feel the warmth on our skin. However, when it is a cloudy day we cannot see the sun or feel the warmth. Does this mean the sun has stopped shining? No the sun is always shining, always – 24 hours a day. It shines when we can't see it behind the clouds and it is shining at night in our opposite hemisphere. The same is true of Pure Light. It is always there and always shining, but if there are blocks between us and Pure Light we will not feel the Light and may even doubt it is there.

Clouds are a physical block that stop us from seeing and feeling the sun, but that doesn't take away any of the sun's power. The sun is just as powerful above the clouds, but we are not feeling it, because there is a block in the way.

If there are blocks between earth and Pure Source Light, such as the ozone layer or other invisible layers of energy, then we won't feel the full power of Pure Light. We will feel cut off from it and start to doubt if it is even there. This is what has happened over many, many years. Layers of energetic blocks have been placed between Pure Source Energy and ourselves, so we can't really feel it that much, and instead we feel the closer energy of dark that has infiltrated earth.

Another way to stop light or sun from shining on a certain place is to reflect or redirect the light. If we hold up a mirror to face the sun or an indoor light, then anywhere under or behind the mirror is not going to receive any light as it gets reflected away and the mirror acts as a physical barrier to the light shining through it. (For those of you who have had many experiences with dark energies, it could answer many questions you have had and raise a few more! It could even be a light-bulb awareness moment for you!)

So even though Light is more powerful than dark, the amount of Light reaching earth has been hugely reduced, allowing dark to do so much evil.

If you feel any fear creeping in after reading this then remember that we can disconnect from fear, and now seems a good time to add more power to our disconnecting statement.

We are going to add in 'Choosing Pure Love & Light', which may sound like nothing, but when you can feel energy, you will feel how powerful this is!

Awaken

Please read this statement three times and notice how you feel.

*"I Choose Pure Love & Light.
Pure Source Energy & the Full Power of the Universe Disconnects Me from Fear Now, and Fills Me with Pure Love and Light and flowing Divine Peace."*

How do you feel?

- Calmer?
- Can you feel energy moving?
- Head shaking, muscle spasms?
- Goose bumps, tingles?
- Hot or cold sensations?
- Feeling old fears or memories coming up?

All of these are quite common, and whatever you do feel is ok, so please don't worry or be alarmed, just support yourself and be kind and proud that you are feeling the energy that is helping to create peace on earth! If you aren't feeling anything yet then that is fine, just keep reading the statements and you will start to feel some sensations creep in.

We are all unique, we have had different lives and experiences and we are going to react to the same situation in different ways.
Anytime you feel fear creeping up on you, please repeat any of the following statements: -

Pure Love, Light & Peace

- Pure Love and Light fill me now and repel all fear
- I choose to disconnect from all fear and fill with Pure Love instead
- I use the Power of the Universe to fill me with Divine energies and disconnect me from vibrations of fear now
- I Choose Pure Love and Light and repel all fear now
- Filling with Pure Love and Light
- Pure Love and Light

Please read through these statements a few times and pick the ones that you most resonate with and make it your choice and habit to use them. You can write them down on a small piece of card and carry them around with your credit cards so that you can refer to them and read them anytime!

Well we have had an introduction to energy, vibrations, Law of Attraction and how to disconnect from fear, so now it's time to go back to our main topic and the title of this book, 'Awaken', and how we can use energy to create Peace on Earth.

Awaken

The Dominant Energy

Many people ask me the following question: -

If Light is more powerful than dark, then why do we have wars, poverty, illness, slavery and all the bad and evil that exists on Earth?

I have also asked myself this question so many times, and I have kept asking it until I have found some answers that made sense to me, because it is a puzzling issue.

Pure Love, Light & Peace

I have even been through phases of discerning and asking the question: -

Is Light more powerful than dark?

Each time the answer has been yes, and I have asked this many times, because it really hasn't felt like Light is more powerful than dark to me when I am seeing, hearing and reading all the dreadful issues that are happening in our world and in the news. Having discerned and got a 'yes' answer hundreds if not thousands of times, and trusting that this must be so, then my next question is: -

Why is there so much evil going on in the world?

Surely if Light is more powerful than dark, it will stop the evil and blast it all away?

It appears not! So again the next question is: -

Well why not? Why is Light not stopping evil?

If Light is more powerful than dark then it would either: -

Stop evil from happening and blast it away,
or
By the Law of Attraction it will repel it.

Awaken

Having discerned that Light IS more powerful than dark, and also seeing that we have wars, disease, poverty and many issues that show Light is not repelling dark from earth, then we need to go deeper and find out what exactly has been going on in the world in terms of energy and vibrations.

In short, there has been a huge shift in people's values and moral standards, which has allowed corruption to creep in and slowly take over. So dark has become the dominant energy without us really noticing, and this has been happening over thousands of years, really being intensified in the last hundred of years with mass agriculture, and big changes in society rules, beliefs and thinking.

If Light was the dominant energy, then evil would be the minority energy with dark being out powered, and eventually by the Law of Attraction (Opposites Repel), evil would be repelled from earth.

As we have wars, poverty, illness, communist control, slavery, rape, abuse and much more, then it is fairly obvious that Light is not the dominant energy.

This is where we can 'Awaken'.

Understanding energy, the Laws of the Universe, and in particular the Law of Attraction, we can change the dominant energy to Light through our thoughts, feelings, intentions and actions. The more people who

Pure Love, Light & Peace

do this, the quicker the global shift to Light will happen.

Imagine if 50% of the population of the world really wanted peace, and chose to take action to create it. That would make the percentage equal, 50:50, but with Light being more powerful then it would be the dominant energy and we would have peace on earth. Is it really that difficult to have 50% of the population wake up and consciously choose Light and peace? I believe not. As a snowball rolls down a hill and gathers momentum, it grows in size, and this is true for any movement as it grows and is spread wider and wider to more and more people.

"I consciously and intentionally Choose Pure Love, Light and Peace to be the dominant power and source energy of our World Now"

I can actually feel huge energy processing going on in my head as I type this statement. Energy is that powerful! We can just read a statement with belief and it will start to work! Having half the world say this statement will shift the world into Love, Light and Peace, so half the population choosing Light will make Light the dominant energy.

When you consider all the suffering that is going on in the world today:

Awaken

Cancer, Ebola virus, Zika virus, AIDS, war, terrorism, bombs, mines, dictatorship, control, slavery, rape, abuse, manipulation, lies, deceit and so on . . .

You have to wonder, is it really that difficult to have the majority of people in the world choose Pure Love, Light and Peace as our dominant energy?

I believe that the majority of people **do** want Love, Light and Peace, so if we all want it, then how come we don't have it?

Here we come to the system!

Pure Love, Light & Peace

Awaken

The System

I am assuming that you *are choosing Pure Love, Light and Peace* or you wouldn't be reading this book, but what we are about to discuss can be a little shocking and can send some people into disbelief, so they shut down and switch off.

Let's start with a release to be open minded to this information, and to feel safe finding out and discovering the Truth, so we can spread Love, Light and Peace to make it our reality on earth now, and to not just keep believing what we've already been programmed to believe.

Pure Love, Light & Peace

"Pure Love and Light release all energies stopping you from feeling and knowing the Truth as you read this information, so you are open to new ideas and beliefs, open to being guided by your inner wisdom from your heart and soul."

Notice I have asked for you to be guided by your inner wisdom from 'your heart and soul' and not your mind. This is because around 90% of what most people believe, is not their beliefs at all, but deep programming from society, parents, teachers, leaders, friends, family, TV adverts, and media etc.

From the moment we are conceived, we are connected to the energy in and around us, with a strong bond to our mother, due to the physical closeness being inside her body. We are collecting energies from the people around us, places our mother visits, energies she is in, so we have already been 'polluted with impure energies of human life' before we have been born! Shocking huh! Well that's just the beginning, because it's downhill from there on for most of us! Once being born, we become apart of the physical world as our own individual being, collecting and storing all the energies from people around us, and the energies they have stored. We also become connected to the mass of global energies or 'collective consciousness' and this happens without us consciously knowing anything about it, after all, we were just a newborn baby!

Awaken

Our parents and teachers have a huge influence on us in our early years. We will subconsciously pick up so many beliefs and patterns from our parents and people closest to us, and will find ourselves repeating many of those beliefs without even knowing it or questioning them.

What did your parents constantly say to you?

- Money doesn't grow on trees
- We can't afford it
- True Love is a fairytale and doesn't exist
- There is no happy ever after
- Life is a struggle
- That's the way it is
- You have to get a degree to be successful

I'm sure you can add many more to the list. How do you feel about these beliefs?

- Are these beliefs inspiring?
- Do they motivate you?
- Do you believe them?

Your head or mind might say yes because you've heard them so often, but what about your heart and soul? How do you *feel* when you read them and connect to them and question them?

The thing is that we have been so programed from birth, to accept everything we were told to be true.

Pure Love, Light & Peace

Many people don't ask questions and challenge what we are told, as we are taught to blindly believe. We really need to start to ask: -

- Is that true?
- Does it make sense?
- Is it morally right?
- Do I want to take on this belief and live by it for the whole of my life?

These are very important questions to ask, and most people don't ask them because we have been programmed by society to just learn, repeat and accept. However it is a very dangerous place to be in where everyone just accepts, and no one is checking that everything is in alignment with good moral values and for the best well being being of all.

This is how dark has crept in; very sneakily and beneath the surface, making one small change at a time so no one will notice, and then building on those changes.

It's like if you want to have a better figure, but you think and focus on all the effort and work involved to change your diet and do a daily exercise routine, you may feel overwhelmed and not start. However, if you just change one thing at a time it will be easier to get started and easier to keep going! Over a period of time those changes will add up and you will not just have a better figure but a healthier lifestyle too.

Awaken

For example, you could decide to replace all refined sugar with molasses, which is a much healthier option, being the original natural plant that hasn't been refined and had all the goodness removed! You are still taking sugar, so no sugar cravings, but a refined product that is very fattening, has been replaced with a natural alternative. You can then add in going for a short walk three to five times a week, which again is fairly easy to do, and you can choose to walk up steps instead of using lifts, and just gradually increase your exercise, without actually going to a gym. You might then decide to change white processed flour for some organic wholemeal flour, which like the sugar isn't changing your diet drastically, but it is improving the healthiness of your diet, without causing any cravings.

If you continue to keep making small changes like this, then over a period of a few years, you will have really improved your diet and health, without any major upset and attention to what is going on.

Well this is exactly what dark has been doing to us, only in reverse! All our healthy natural products have slowly been replaced with processed artificial ones, which have chemicals added to them, that make us crave them, even though they cause us to put on weight, have bad teeth and feel ill!

Farming was taken away from family farmers and made into a huge industrialized process, using many chemicals to speed everything up and create more profits.

Small towns and family shops were taken over by large shopping centres, and many towns lost their community spirit in the process. Remember the days or seen it in movies, where communities all work together and look after each other, providing gifts and helping out when someone in the community needed it? How much of that goes in big cities? It doesn't, because people have been programmed to lose their sense of compassion and caring, and with it important moral values have disappeared too.

If we had all known from the outset that large companies were planning to take over our food and fill it with toxic chemicals that are causing and creating so many illnesses, would we have just silently let it happen? No of course not, but it was done one small step at a time so we didn't notice. If anyone does notice and says anything, then they are ridiculed and made to appear crazy so no one will listen to them.

When we start to awaken, we can see that it is not just with our food that this switch from natural to toxic chemicals has happened, the switch from pure to evil has and still is happening in all areas of our lives.

When we dig deeper we can see that we are being controlled by dark intentions, as they buy out the small companies and replace them with fewer large companies. We have been sold this as a positive for us, but it is actually reducing the choice we have, as these larger companies have control over the whole show and smaller companies go out of business because they can't compete on price, and we are left with no alternative than these big companies.

This is true for:

- Finance – The 'Big Banks' are in control
- Health – FDA controls all drugs and patents of new drugs
- Vaccines contain toxic chemicals and are being made compulsory in some countries
- Education – children are programmed to sit still, be quiet, learn and repeat information, to be part of the system, without questioning what is really going on
- Food – is being genetically modified and sprayed with toxic chemicals
- Politics – world leaders are influenced behind the scenes by money and hidden agendas
- Military – wars create dark energy and profit for dark agendas, fear for the masses and reduces the population of caring souls
- Chemtrails – toxic chemicals filling our skies, which pollutes our soil, water and food chain each time it rains
- Energy – Oil and fossil fuels have created great wealth for a minority, controlling us through high prices. When we have 'free natural

energy' available to all – solar, wind, wave and many more amazing technologies are being invented but not being fully used now – why not?
- Media – Major channels are all controlled behind the scenes to create mass fear and keep us in the dark and controlled
- Check out alternative stations and find out the Truth!

There is much information available on all of the above subjects, so I am not going to expand on this, because my gifts and talents lie with energy healing and channeling energy. You can find out more from those who have done the research, just as I did myself. We all do need to expand our view of life, to know and learn more about what is actually going on around us, and to know the Truth about our world. If the masses don't wake up to the Truth soon, then a small minority will continue to destroy our world until there is nothing left – when we 'Awaken' we can choose 'Peace' and spread and share how peace can be created.

I chose the title of 'Awaken' because through learning the Truth of what is happening to our world and the people on it, we can become motivated to take action to stop this craziness. How much action you choose is your choice, it needs to fit in with you and your lifestyle. Whatever you do, no matter how small, is

Awaken

sending out 'peace ripples' into the world, so please know what you do does count and that you count.

When we decide to find out more, we need to make sure that we are connecting with good energy and getting correct information. With the Internet, there is so much information out there, and as we discover that nearly everything we once believed is not true, how can we believe or trust anything?

How do we know what is true?

Well that is another great question and brings us to our next chapter, another very important topic – discerning, which is 'knowing what is Truth'.

Pure Love, Light & Peace

Discerning the Truth

How can we discern what is Truth? Well there is actually a very simple and easy way to do this and that is through our feelings.

'Wisdom and Truth' are felt through our feelings.

This is great news, because while it is easy, or has been easy, for people to con and manipulate us through our minds with false beliefs, it's not so easy for anyone to change our deep inner feelings, that come from our soul connection, Divine energies, the Universe and Divine Truth.

Pure Love, Light & Peace

When we are connected to Divine Truth through our soul connection, then we feel and know the Truth.

Our soul connection is in our stomach / abdominal area, and well, you know that 'kicked in the gut' feeling? That is your soul talking to you! When this feeling is super strong we feel it, but when it isn't so strong, and we're caught up in every day human life, the rat race, earning money to pay bills and exist, then we aren't tuned in and paying attention to our feelings. The important messages from our soul don't get through to us because we are so wrapped up in the 'stress of life'.

Being tuned into our soul connection and soul guidance is called discerning. This is Divine Source letting us know what is Truth and what is not. This includes giving us messages as to what is in Divine Integrity, what will keep us in integrity and in Divine Flow, and what is taking us off track and into dark and low vibrations that cause illness, lack, arguments, and all the issues we don't want.

So you may well be wondering, how do we discern and have this information flow to us? Which takes us to our next chapter – How to Discern.

How to Discern

To be able to discern we do need a strong connection to our soul, and we will discuss that later, but first let's talk about discerning and how we do it. When you try it for yourself you will be able to feel how connected your soul is or isn't if you're not getting very clear results.

Discerning is all about feeling. In the western world we are very much programmed to think, and are programmed that feelings are ridiculous, crazy, fairytales, woo-woo and many more things.

Pure Love, Light & Peace

However in our modern society, we actually have it all backwards! Those that live close to nature, all the natives in the world, live through their feelings, tuning into Divine Source, nature and living through instinct and trust. Being in Divine Flow is doing just this, living through feelings, instinct and trust.

To feel we need to quieten our minds and switch off all the mind chatter. This is simple to type, and equally simple to read, however actually achieving this and feeling stillness and silence in our mind is not always an easy task, especially for those people who have such busy schedules and are always dashing and rushing around.

So let's start with working on our mind, and how we can silence the mind chatter, and have some moments of stillness. To start with, reaching just a moment of stillness, will be an amazing feeling, and a huge achievement; so do be patient and kind to yourself as you experiment with this!

Just read through this statement, taking in the information so you can do this again with your eyes closed. If you can't remember it all then that's ok, just read it with your eyes open and feel stillness and quiet in your mind as you do read it: -

"I ask Divine Peace to fill and flow to your mind now, Filling your mind with Divine Peace."
Take a few deep breaths, close your eyes, and

Awaken

Let all mind chatter just float away and feel peace and stillness. Allow this feeling of peace and stillness to stay with you as you connect to your feelings."

I hope that you are feeling calmer, quieter, and have more inner peace now. If you aren't then please do read the statement again, a few more times, until you do feel some peace and stillness in your mind. This is really important, as you are not going to be able to discern clearly, if you have 101 thoughts whizzing around inside your head!

Once we are feeling some stillness in our minds, we need to focus on what we wish to discern, and how we are going to do this.

To discern we ask a question that is going to give a clear 'yes or no' answer. If you don't phrase the question clearly to give a yes or no answer, then you will not get a clear answer! There are a few main reasons why people have some issues with discerning clearly: -

- The question isn't asked in a clear and concise way to give a yes / no answer
- The person is too in their head and mind chatter to feel an answer
- The person has blocks to their soul connection which is preventing them from receiving a clear answer

Pure Love, Light & Peace

- The person doesn't really want to know the answer and is sabotaging the process!

To start we need to think of a question to ask. Let's start with something that is easy and that you know the answer to instantly, without any doubt. Then we can work out how we can phrase the question to give a clear yes / no answer.

So the question is: - 'Is my name . . . . ' (where you insert your name)

The phrasing of that question is **simple** and **clear,** and the answer is going to be **yes** or **no**.

Place your attention on your stomach, for a gut feeling or your heart area, and ask this question and notice what you feel.

If you feel a rising feeling, a lightening feeling, feeling good, happy, or uplifted, then this indicates a 'yes' or 'true' answer.

If you feel a lowering feeling, a heavy, down, depressed, not good or a sinking feeling then the answer is 'no' or 'false'.

So what did you feel? Was it the right answer? Or maybe you didn't feel anything, which is quite normal when people start to learn to discern. It is a skill that needs lots of practice, like playing a musical instrument or art, the more we practice the better we get at it. So ask again a few more times and notice what you feel.

As you practice more and more, and try with different questions that you know the answer to, like 'Do I live in England' (or wherever you live), you will become more tuned in and find it easier to feel the answer. If you don't start to feel more tuned in, this is an indication of some soul barriers, which again is quite normal and we can do energy work to release them, which we will discuss later.

You may get different feelings from the ones I have listed above, and that is ok, as long as you clearly know what your feelings are for a yes and no answer. Remember to ask questions that are going to give you a 'no' answer as well as yes, so you can tune into what this feeling is.

I have a strong soul connection, and my head will physically and visibly nod for a yes and shake for a no. Sometimes the feeling will be more subtle, especially if I'm asking a question in a public place, where I don't' want to look like I'm insane!

Once you know your feelings for a yes and no answer, you can then start to ask questions that you don't know the answer for, and see what you feel for those. Yay, exciting stuff!

Pure Love, Light & Peace

The questions need to be connected to Divine Truth. If you ask questions like, 'which colour is prettier red or blue?', then you won't get a clear answer. Firstly, the question hasn't been phrased to give a yes or no answer, and secondly, because there is no Truth for this question, it is a matter of personal preference.

Keep practicing and working on asking questions and your intuition, guidance and ability to discern will improve and start to serve you well. You can ask if a job opportunity is in your best interests, and in alignment with your heart, soul and true inner desires. Also, if a person, company, or project have Divine intention and your best interests at heart, and so on. Discerning is a way to keep you connected to Pure energies, people with high morals and Divine integrity. It also keeps you out of trouble and connecting to people, places, groups, jobs and circumstances that are going to drag you down into lower energies.

Remember these guidelines for your questions: -

- It needs to give an answer that is connected to Truth not preference
- You need to phrase your question simply and clearly to give a yes or no answer
- The answer is a feeling!
- If you're not feeling an answer then quieten your mind and try again

- Practice is needed to improve. Each question will bring you closer to strong discernment, so keep going!

As a quick and simple double check, there is another very simple way to discern if a belief is 'The Truth' or not, and it is to ask, 'does this belief make you and others happy, loved and supported'? If it does then it will be from Pure Source and will be a true belief. If it causes any upset, trauma or negative emotions in you or others, then the belief or action is not from Pure Source Energy and is not of Pure intention.

What if you are doing all of the above and are still not feeling any answers? This is an indication that you have some blocks and barriers to feeling your soul connection, which means that we need to do some releasing energy work to shift those blocks, so you can feel much clearer and more easily.

Pure Love, Light & Peace

Awaken

Soul Barriers & Blocks to Feeling

If you have been asking the discerning questions and have not been feeling anything, then I'm sure you're feeling pretty frustrated, so let's dive right in with a release, and we can chat about the rest afterwards!

"Pure Love & Light releases all blocks, barriers and energies preventing you from being connected to your soul, feeling discernment and your soul guidance. Sending all energies released direct to source, and Filling with Divine Truth and Pure Light."

Pure Love, Light & Peace

You may well feel some strong sensations whilst or after reading that statement, you may feel dizzy or light-headed, or feel some cramps, or other feelings in your stomach area. This is quite normal and will be the blocking energies moving out, so you can have a clearer connection to your soul.

In my book, Loving You – Discover Your True Inner Self, I talk about layers of energy covering our inner diamond or true, Pure source self. In 'Loving You', I am talking about our heart energy and layers that build up around our heart, to stop us feeling loved, and sharing love. These heart barriers usually accumulate when we do not feel loved, from birth or early childhood, and we continue to collect these magnets more and more, as they become the more dominant magnet in our energy.

You may have noticed that everything has an opposite:

- Feeling loved, feeling unloved
- Love and hate
- Rich and poor
- Worthy and not good enough and so on

When we have a feeling it is either one or the other of these feelings. We don't feel loved and unloved at exactly the same time, so we are collecting magnets for the feeling, emotion or belief that we are experiencing in that moment. The more of each particular emotion or feeling we have stored in us, and the longer we spend feeling this emotion, will determine how many more of these 'like magnets' will be attracted, collected and stored within us.

For example if we have felt unloved all our lives and therefore collected many 'unloved magnets' and at age 30 something happens that triggers us to feel unloved, then with 30 years of stored unloved magnets inside us, we are going to be triggered quite a bit, and attract a lot more unloved magnets to us. The longer we dwell in this feeling, the more we will attract unwanted magnets, until we can change what we are feeling to a more positive emotion.

I hope you can see from this, that is it very important to be aware of our feelings, and also of what emotions and beliefs we have stored in us, so we can prevent and stop the cycle of attracting more and more unwanted and negative magnets to us.

There may be times with the above example where we do feel loved, but as we won't have many 'feeling loved magnets' stored in us, we will not be able to attract many of these magnets to us. We cannot attract what we don't already have inside us, so if someone doesn't feel loved at all, then they may well find it almost impossible to really feel and connect to emotions of Pure love.

We are going to have a dominant energy or magnet for nearly every belief or emotion we have connected with during our lives, which will be either a Pure magnet or a dark one. The dominant or strongest magnet will be attracting more at a greater rate than the weaker magnet, because we already have more of those magnets stored in us. This happens even if we don't want it to, unless we do some powerful energy work to release the magnets we don't want. This is because the power of the energy of feelings is more powerful than our thoughts. In fact, science is now showing that our heart energy and emotions are 5,000 times more powerful than our thoughts, so if you have ever tried affirmations and they've not worked for you, you now know why not!

We cannot con our feelings.

If an affirmation or statement doesn't feel true to us, then it will not ring true and work for us like it would if we believed it was true for us.

Anyone who has given themselves a hard time for not succeeding through affirmations now needs to give themselves a big hug and realize that was not your fault, it's an incomplete system.

Affirmations will work if you feel them to be true for you. You may need to rephrase them so there isn't an instant clash, as you feel the 'that's not true' as you read it!

Awaken

For example, if you don't believe this statement below: -

'I love my body, my body is thin and attractive.'

Then you can rephrase it to: -

'I love all the cells in my body and I desire my body to look and be thin and attractive.'

If you are not happy with your figure then the first affirmation is going to scream not true to you! Rephrasing it stops this from happening, and means you will accept the statement and the positive message, because you have no reason to not love the cells in your body and you do desire your body to look good.

I've kind of gone off topic there a bit, but I trust you will find that information enlightening and very useful, especially if you've been using affirmations and they've not been working for you!

So back to these barriers; we can have invisible energetic barriers or layers around our heart that stop us from feeling love and we also can have them around our soul, stopping us from feeling Divine Truth, integrity, intuition and natural instinct.

When we remove these barriers we are open to feel more easily, to flow with nature, the universe and Divine flow.

Pure Love, Light & Peace

Another point about feelings versus thoughts is, it can be easy for a well trained sales person to talk us into something, i.e. change our mind from saying we don't want to buy something, to agreeing to buy it, even when we may still not really want it!

On an even deeper level, trained people can mess with our beliefs and brainwash us into believing something that isn't true. This is how cults can work, and how society has changed from the small town caring communities, to the large dehumanized cities. This has happened very subtly, over many years, so we don't notice it. When someone does notice and speaks out, they are ridiculed and put down, people are trained to follow the masses, and are blinded to the Truth, so our world keeps getting more and more polluted, toxic, and controlled by a select few.

When we are in tune with our feelings, it is much harder for someone to pull the wool over our eyes, and to con us, because we can instantly *feel* that it is not right, not true, and not good for us, or society, nature and our world.

The more we tune into our feelings, the more it becomes totally natural and just happens, like walking, we don't consciously think about how to walk, and it becomes the same with feeling, we just feel.

When I'm deciding what to wear in the morning, I am using my feelings – what would I feel good wearing

Awaken

today? I am very influenced by colours. Every now and then when clothes shopping I might *think* I should expand my wardrobe to include more colours that I don't usually wear; but then when I'm home and actually choosing what to wear, I don't *feel* I want to wear the new colour and so they don't get worn! So my *head* has said you need to have a bigger choice of colours of clothes, then when I come to wear them, my *feelings* say 'I don't want to wear that colour!'

This is having an imbalance or disagreement between our head and our heart, thoughts versus feelings. It is actually very common with most people having their heads in control, and whenever they do go into their feelings, then the mind butts back in and takes control again!

My solution to this issue would be to use my feelings when I am shopping, and ask myself 'do I feel like I want to wear this colour?' If my answer is no, then it's unlikely I will change how I feel after I have bought the garment, and taken it home. This of course applies to all areas of our lives; we all need to use our feelings so much more, to decide through feeling, what is the best choice for us.

Once we break free of this mind control, and we are living mainly through our feelings, then we instinctively feel the energy around us, other people's energy, whether someone is trying to con us or not, and life does become a lot clearer and easier. So when the well

Pure Love, Light & Peace

trained sales person is trying to sell us something we don't want, or to con us with something that is not good, i.e. a car with dodgy brakes, then we will feel that this is not good for us, and we won't allow ourselves to be pulled in by the sales talk. It can take a while to be this open to feeling, but if you keep releasing the blocks and barriers and choose to live through 'feeling' rather than mind control, then your feelings will become this tuned in. (Then, of course, we do have to trust our feelings, because the next stage is that we feel the feelings, and then let our minds talk us out of going with them and trusting them!)

You may be wondering how our feelings can be so powerful to give us this information, so let's go back to the Law of Attraction with: -

'Like Attracts Like and Opposites Repel.'

As you tune into feeling, you will have more 'feeling magnets' stored in you and so you will repel vibrations that are mind controlled, which are opposite energies to feeling and intuition. We are either following our intuition, or being controlled by our minds, we cannot do both in the same moment.

Each moment of life can be a choice between Choosing the Pure or the dark option.

Once we have chosen through our feelings, we can then use our minds to work out the finer details, admin, schedules etc. and this is not a dark choice, because our minds are designed to do the finer scheduling, mathematics and all the details. All our main choices and decisions should come through our heart, soul and our feelings, to be Pure and in alignment with Divine integrity.

This is an incredibly important skill for life and living, when people are tuned into their feelings we will have a society of kind, caring, and compassionate people wishing to work together for the good of the whole and supporting each other.

Remember the small towns where everyone will chip in and work together during a crisis or when a family needs help? Well this is our heart energy and compassion at work. We will have a much higher vibration world when people live through their feelings, and a much lower vibration world when people are dictated to through mind control; look at the dreadful wars and events that have happened through mass mind dictatorship.

Pure Love, Light & Peace

Awaken

How We Have Been Conned

If we wish to 'Create Peace on Earth,' with humanity living harmoniously together again, we need to know how we have been conned. If we don't know that we are being conned, then nothing is going to change. It is through seeing the true reality of what is happening in the world that we are able to 'awaken' and say this is wrong and this is not what we want. The more people who awaken to see the Truth, then the easier it is for this new united viewpoint to work together to create Love, Light and Peace.

We have chatted about disconnecting from fear, so if you feel any fear creep in at anytime whilst reading

Pure Love, Light & Peace

this book, or in your life then please disconnect from it. It is simple to do and only takes a few seconds: -

"I disconnect from this fear now."

Or

"Pure Love & Light disconnects me from this fear now."

Or

"Pure Source Energy / The Power of the Universe Disconnects me from this fear now."

When we look at living through our feelings it is a very open, honest and transparent way to live. You cannot lie to anyone because they will feel it is a lie, and you will be found out.

We have been conned by disconnecting us from: -

- Our feelings and authentic way of living
- Feeling the Truth and knowing when something is wrong
- Living an open, honest life
- Choosing through morals and feelings to support others
- Choosing kindness and compassion to support others

Instead we have been programmed through mind control to: -

Awaken

- Follow the system, 'do as others do'
- Not feel, not be compassionate, not care, not question
- Tick the boxes of the system and defend it to the end
- Ridicule anyone who opts out of the system
- Be heartless and cruel to victims, homeless etc.
- Act more like robots than 'hearts and souls' in a human body

Isn't this shocking?

By making small changes over and over again, the majority of the 'civilized' population has been de-sensitized to caring about each other to some extent or other.

In all areas of our lives we are being programmed to not care, not question, not be in tune with our feelings, and to not take action when we know something is wrong. We are being filled with fear to stop us taking action, along with the belief that we are so insignificant against the whole system / governments etc. that we have no power and we can't change what is going on. However this is not true. All the wrong doing and conning is being done by a very small percentage of the population. The majority of people in the world are still kind, caring and compassionate underneath all the mind programming,

Pure Love, Light & Peace

and when awakened souls choose Pure over evil, then huge change happens.

> *We all do actually have 'Free Choice' and*
> *We can choose.*

We can choose to: -

- Check out the facts
- Discern and feel what feels good for us
- Chat to like minded people and share views
- Join groups that are promoting positive change, that have no political agenda, and are working to create a greener, cleaner more natural world
- Disconnect from fear
- Become Energy Aware
- Choose Pure over evil and to choose not to play their game!

Awaken

Don't Play the Game!

We can choose to opt out of the game, the system of being controlled and treated like a robot in the factory of life – oh yes we can!

It takes a while to realize, believe and know that we are being conned so much, and trapped in a system that isn't serving us, but when we realize this and then choose to opt out it gives us freedom!

To opt out of the game we need to learn the Truth to see and know what is going on. This can create a bit of fear in some people so it is important that we disconnect from fear before we start to seek out the

Pure Love, Light & Peace

Truth, and keep disconnecting from fear whenever we do feel fear anywhere in our lives. Remember that fear is power for dark so we don't want to be feeling fear at all, and we can disconnect from it with determined action. This is why I explained how to disconnect from fear at the beginning of this book, so you can really take it on board and get to work with achieving it!

Now we need to look at this in more detail and understand the process in terms of energy. This allows us to see how it works and why it is so important to disconnect from fear, and any other energies that aren't serving us or making us feel good. We can actually disconnect from any feeling or belief that we want to, it is all just a question of knowledge and choosing to do it.

Let's go back to energy. We have chatted that emotions have opposites and that we collect either the Pure or dark, and that we cannot collect both at the same time. One emotion will be more dominant and more powerful and will control how we react to other energy and emotions connecting to us. If our internal emotions are equal, (which can happen as we release the negative low emotion and fill with the higher Pure emotion); then the emotion that we feel, will be the dominant emotion or energy outside of us, that is the global energy surrounding us at that moment of time.

We do need to talk more about this global or collective energy, which is all the energy of everyone and everything in the world, stored as a massive powerful group of magnets that affect us.

We have our single energy field and then there is the energy of everyone and everything else in the whole world. Which is going to have more power, the world or us? Logically the answer points to the world just on volume and this is usually true, which is why we need to 'opt out' or disconnect from the global energy. If we don't disconnect from the global energy, then it is controlling your life without you knowing it. (Such as always being attracted to the wrong partner, even when you're intending to break the pattern, is one example of how much your life is being controlled by global magnets.)

A thought that just popped into my head is that, you may not realize and understand that when we are disconnecting or releasing, we are only disconnecting or releasing the low, dark, evil and damaging energies. All the Pure vibrations exist naturally and they stay, so disconnecting from the global energy or 'collective consciousness' is stopping those negative beliefs and emotions from triggering our internal magnets and creating havoc with our lives! All the good and Pure exists naturally, so there is no need to worry that disconnecting will stop the good flowing, it doesn't! In fact, with the bad gone it flows more easily and freely!

Let's have a visual image for this. Imagine that all our internal magnets, (emotions, beliefs, etc.) are the size of a penny coin and that all the energies in the whole world are the size of a massive football stadium, and both have magnet energy. If the dominant magnet energy of the world is low, dark and evil then our little penny size magnet is trying to work against, and out power a massive football stadium magnet – fair contest? Not at all! We are totally out powered. However, if we disconnect from the football stadium magnet, then we regain the power in our own penny magnet!

In terms of the world energy, when we disconnect from the global magnets or collective consciousness, with all the dark magnets lurking there, then we have total free choice and freedom to live our lives as we desire, without having any interference from outside magnets.

The global magnet is actually millions of different magnets, affecting all areas of our lives, so we are unknowingly being very controlled by the magnetic pull of this collective magnetic energy unless we disconnect from it.

As we disconnect from the collective consciousness more and more, we strengthen our connection to Pure Source, our Divine integrity, intuition and inner knowing. With Light being more powerful than dark, we will get our personal power back! Not only that, but as we join forces with other Light souls and create our own 'Light magnet' or 'Light Consciousness', our

Awaken

collective Light energy will increase and eventually 'out power' the whole of the current dark global magnet.

This is how we can create peace on earth.

It is not only possible; it is doable, because it is using the Power of the Universe to our advantage. For centuries now the dominant energy on earth has been dark and evil, so the Law of Attraction has been working against most people, attracting more dark and evil into their lives such as lack, hurt, trauma and victim magnets.

When we disconnect from all of the dark and victim magnets, we are literally emitting higher frequencies that connect us to Pure Source; bringing good into our lives, synchronicity and Divine Flow, which can connect us to other like minded souls, so together we unite in creating a new way of living on earth that involves natural energy and resources and creates, Love, Light, Peace, Joy and Abundance for All!

When we know, feel and believe this we feel excited and inspired! We want to share this information with others so they can join in and help to create a better way of living.

I mean haven't we all suffered enough already? There are so many people who are really stuck in desperate places, we really do need to do all we can to help them. So this brings us to another really important question: —

What can I do to make a difference?

Awaken

What Can I do to Make a Difference?

I hear so many people say they can't do anything to help, they are just themselves, one person, and they have no ability or power to create change against governments, illuminati, new world order and all the evil that is going on.

Well if you were just one isolated person then that would be true, but you are not just one isolated person, you are a part of the collective consciousness of the world. Each time someone chooses to disconnect from the current collective consciousness and chooses instead to unite their intention with those choosing Pure Love, Light and Peace, it increases the power of this new collective energy, which we will call Light Consciousness.

Let's go back to the huge global 'football stadium' magnet that is global consciousness, where we are a penny magnet inside that football stadium magnet, along with all the other penny magnets making up the whole massive football stadium. If half of the penny magnets are released or disconnect from the football stadium then the stadium is now half as powerful as it was. So this action has hugely decreased the power of the global energy, but on top of that all those penny magnets that left the stadium have now created a new football stadium of Light Consciousness. As Light IS more powerful than dark, then the new Light football stadium out powers the old dark one!

It is not a question of: -

Is it possible to create Peace on Earth and live through kindness and compassion?

It is a question of: -

How long is it going to take for enough people to 'Awaken'.

Each person who chooses to leave the dark global consciousness to choose peace and be a part of the new Light Consciousness is making a difference, and is helping to switch the dominant power from dark to Light on earth now.

So now that you have all this new information from reading this book, along with any other research you may do, you now have a choice, you can: -

- Do nothing - leaving your personal power where it currently is, in the collective consciousness, which is supporting dark and all the evil that is going in our world

- Choose to disconnect from the dark consciousness - choose Pure Love & Light, taking your personal power away from the dark consciousness, giving you freedom for your own personal life, and adding Light power to the world, shifting the whole world into Love, Light and Peace

What we haven't been told is that we are automatically added to a collective consciousness when we are born. Since this collective currently has a dominant dark energy controlling it, we are by default connected to being controlled by dark without knowing it unless we 'intentionally and consciously choose Pure Light Consciousness.'

Doing this is actually very easy in principle, but is something that needs to be done repeatedly to be effective like cleaning our teeth; it's not a 'one in a lifetime event'!

'I intentionally and consciously choose Pure Light Consciousness'

There are many levels to disconnecting, and you can decide how deep you want to go. I will walk you through this process in the next chapter, and the simplest level is to just read the statements in the next chapter with emotion and add your intention to choose Pure Light Consciousness.

The next level of choosing is to repeat these statements every day, or as often as you can, like a daily prayer, to really disconnect yourself from the dark consciousness and add your energy to Light Consciousness. Now doing this is not only going to help raise the vibration of the world and help create a new way of living on earth, which will benefit us all, but it will also hugely improve your life. As you reduce your connection to dark magnets and increase your connection to Light magnets your life will change for the better! You will attract less bad into your life and more good, this will happen by the Power of the Universe and the Law of Attraction. Yes it really does work when we're not connected to all those dark magnets!

You may have watched the film 'The Secret' and tried to think or affirm your way to manifesting the life you desired, and like many didn't succeed. This is because the energy magnets we have stored inside us are far more powerful than the power of our minds, or even the power of our feelings, (which are 5,000 times more powerful than our thoughts).

To demonstrate the 'Power of the Laws of the Universe', let's take the 'Law of Gravity', which is the magnetic attraction of all objects to earth, i.e. anything not supported will fall downwards.

If it was possible to manifest with our thoughts and mind power only then we should be able to say, chant, affirm that a pen will stay floating in the air when we let it go. Well I think we have all dropped enough pens in our time to know that the Law of Gravity is pretty powerful, and that all the chanting and affirming in the world isn't going to out power it!

To create peace and make a world filled with love, Light, compassion and abundance for all, we need to use the most powerful energy source we can, and that is not our mind power, it is Pure Source Energy, Pure Love and Light or the Power of the Universe, depending on which name you wish to use.

Scientific data from NASA has shown that the resonance of earth dropped noticeably during and after the attacks on New York on 9/11. The shock, trauma and grief being felt worldwide, as people

Pure Love, Light & Peace

watched this horrific event on TVs around the world, was enough to lower the vibration of the whole world.

If negative energies lower the vibration of the world, then positive or Pure energies will raise the vibration of the world. When we focus our attention and energy on choosing Pure over evil, and disconnecting from fear, we are creating a higher vibration world with kinder, caring energies being the dominant energies.

All this can be done from your home without any real inconvenience or expense from you. So let's make a start and learn what we need to say to create this shift NOW!

Awaken

The Power of Free Choice Choosing Light

So let's jump right in with some statements to read, to use our power of 'Free Choice' to choose Light Consciousness.

"I use my power of free choice to consciously and intentionally choose Pure Light Consciousness."

"I use the Power of the Universe and my power of free choice to consciously and intentionally choose Pure Light Consciousness."

Pure Love, Light & Peace

"I use the Power of the Universe and my power of free choice to consciously and intentionally disconnect from the collective consciousness and to choose Pure Light Consciousness."

If you can feel energy, then you most probably felt energy shifting as you read those statements, such as light-headed, dizzy, spaced etc. This is how many people do feel energy and is quite normal. If you didn't feel anything then that is fine, you have still made a difference just by reading these statements, and you will continue to make a difference each and every time you read them again. The more you do read them, the more likely you are to feel the energy and power in them. When this happens and you can really feel the energy moving, you will **know** you are making a difference, and this will inspire you to keep making a difference, and share the power of doing this with everyone you connect with who is open to hearing it!

We can increase the power in the above statements by adding more energy to them: -

"I Use The Power of the Universe, The Power Of Pure Love, The Power Of Pure Light And My Power Of Free Choice To Choose Pure Light Consciousness."

"I Use The Power of the Universe, The Power Of Pure Love, The Power Of Pure Light And My Power Of Free Choice, To Disconnect From The Collective

Awaken

Consciousness, and To Choose Pure Light Consciousness."

Again when you can feel energy you will feel and notice that these statements are more powerful, and you will feel more energy shifting. If you are wondering what 'energy shifting' means, then it is moving the energy from one collective to another one, i.e. from dark to Light.

Pure Love, Light & Peace

Disconnecting from Mind Control

Let's use a visual example to help really understand what is happening when we disconnect from mind control or 'collective consciousness'.

Imagine we have two pools full of balls. One pool has black balls in it, and the other pool has white balls in it. The black ball pool represents our current collective consciousness and is all the global energy in the world. We are by default connected to this as soon as we are born or conceived. The black pool has been and is predominantly under the control of dark energy.

Pure Love, Light & Peace

The white ball pool is the new Light Consciousness that is being created as people choose to disconnect from the current collective, to choose Pure Love, Light and Peace.

When we read the disconnecting statements above it is the equivalent of taking black balls out of the black pool and asking 'Pure Source Light' to purify them so they become white balls, and then putting them into the white ball pool.

This visual image is a little over simplified, as it is a huge leap to take a person's whole energy and to totally purify it to be Pure Light with just a few statements, but it gives a general overview of the situation.

A more accurate image would be to imagine the 'collective consciousness' as a large pool of many balls, ranging in colours from black through all the shades of grey to Pure white. Each ball is a vibration for everything that exists on earth, so there are magnets or balls for every emotion, feeling, thought, belief, illness, law, building, group of people, company and so on. The colour of these balls will depend on the vibration of the energy, emotion, belief etc. Very low energies will be dark grey or black such as hate, severe depression, feeling suicidal, controlling beliefs and vibrations that create war, rape and abuse. Pure emotions of love, peace, joy, happiness, laughter, and sharing will be white along with kindness, compassion, and caring. So I'm sure you are getting the picture that everything that exists has a vibration, which has a value, and in our example, it will represent a colour between white and black ranging from totally Pure to evil.

When we do releasing energy work we are changing the vibrations inside us from dark shades to lighter shades, which will make our overall vibration and colour lighter too.

When we disconnect from vibrations in the ball pool, we are stopping them from affecting and influencing our lives. For example, if you have a fear or addiction, you will find it much easier to move out of this fear or addiction if you disconnect from the energy of everyone else with that same fear or addiction in the world. I mean it is challenging enough to deal with your own issues, without having the energy of other people feeding into your issues!

When we choose to disconnect from collective consciousness and choose Light consciousness, what we are doing is getting out of that ball pool, filled with so many mixed magnets that are causing chaos in our lives, and choosing to get into a clearer and purer pool that has been purified, and is filled with Divine and good.

As we get out of the current collective consciousness we are making it smaller and reducing the overall power of it. Choosing Light instead is creating a new stronger, purer power in the new Light Consciousness, which will shine on to the old collective and dissolve and purify as many magnets as possible, making it lighter and higher vibration for those still in it. This means that it will be harder for evil to be the dominant energy of world, as more and more Light is shined on to it. As the world fills with more and more Light then evil by the 'Power of the Universe' and the 'Law of Attraction' will be repelled.

Each person is in the collective consciousness unless they choose to leave it, and this is our 'Free Choice'. The more people who become aware and choose Light over dark, then the more the dominant energy of the world will shift from dark to Light. This is already happening, and with even more awareness we can really speed up this process and create peace on earth.

So each person in the world can and does make a difference, because their views, choices and energy are either supporting the positive shift to Light and Peace or not. Many people would be supporting peace and Light if they knew and understood energy, but the programing and beliefs from society is so great that some just see the power of energy as fairytales, hippy stuff or just crazy. However, when you are aware, what is crazy is not doing anything, not taking any action, and allowing evil to continue to control our lives!

Awaken

How Can We All Make A Difference?

There are many ways we can all make a difference, but one of the easiest and simplest is to read the statements in this book, to choose Pure Love & Light, and disconnect from the collective consciousness.

In fact, each and every time we read these statements we are doing a little bit more energy work to change the dominant world energy from dark to Light.

Every action adds up and makes a difference, just like if you were to put a penny in a jar every day, then at the end of the year you will have 365 pennies in the jar, which is noticeably more than not doing this. If we then decided to put two pennies into the jar a day, then after a year we will have 730 pennies. The same affect applies to how many times a day we read the statements, the more times we read them, the more energy it is shifting!

Another way we can increase the power of what we are doing is to really use our heart and soul intention, and our emotions as we read the statements. When we connect to how much we would like the world to change, and feel those emotions, just before we read the statements, we will increase the power considerably. Remember emotions are 5,000 times more powerful than thoughts!

There are two main ways you can connect to your feelings and emotions, you can either: -

- Feel the bad and evil that is going on in the world and use your upset and anger to add more power to the statement as you read it

- Or to focus on the good feelings of how much better your life will be, or the lives of those who are currently stuck in lack, poverty, war zones, child slave labour, and how great it will be to lift these people out of these dreadful lives, into lives that are happy, where they feel

Awaken

>loved and cared for, and where the world system really does support them

When you next feel really angry or upset about world issues you can use or channel these feelings into creating shift from dark to Light. If you're not sure how to do this then give it a try now.

Read one of the statements below. (It will be more powerful if you read it out loud, but you can read it silently to yourself if you prefer.)

"I Use The Power of the Universe, The Power Of Pure Love, The Power Of Pure Light And My Power Of Free Choice To Choose Pure Light Consciousness."

"I Use The Power of the Universe, The Power Of Pure Love, The Power Of Pure Light And My Power Of Free Choice To Disconnect From The Collective Consciousness And To Choose Pure Light Consciousness."

Then connect to something about the world that makes you really angry, such as child slave labour, forced marriages, rape, war, or whatever issues that create an intense feeling in you, and then read the statement again, allowing all of your anger to flow into the statement. You will most likely feel different as you do this, and it will allow more energy to shift, and therefore it is an excellent way to use negative emotions to create a positive shift!

Pure Love, Light & Peace

This will work anytime you feel angry, or feel any negative emotion, so if something has happened that has left you feeling angry or emotional, you can release these emotions by reading the above statements, allowing your feelings to be channeled into creating a better world – now isn't that amazing!

There are many ways we can all make a difference, so let's make a list of all the ways we can think of. You can make your own list, with ways that appeal to you and then keep referring back to it for inspiration! You can chat to friends, family, people at school, work, clubs and come up with some more amazing ways you can, in small ways, make a difference, such as doing charity work, helping neighbours, smiling at people in the street and so on.

Here are some ways we can make a difference using our energy: -

- To Choose Pure Love & Light
- Disconnect from the Collective Consciousness
- Affirm your Light Consciousness daily with the choosing statements
- Cleanse your own energy with releasing energy work
- Fill your own energy with Pure Divine Energies so you are feeling these Pure energies in your life
- Send Pure Love, Light & Peace out to the World Daily

Awaken

- Send Pure energy to global issues that you hear about on the news
- Send Pure energy to creating World Peace
- Share your beliefs with others
- Encourage others to read this book and become awakened to the power of energy!

Ways we can make a difference in our physical lives: -

- Charity & volunteer work
- Be kind to people, be caring and compassionate
- Do things you love, this keeps you in a good mood!
- Escape the 'box of society' - stop being a human robot!
- Recycling waste / garbage
- Being aware about what we buy, the packaging and contents
- Support companies that support Light Consciousness
- Stop buying from companies that are controlling us
- Choose 'green and renewable energy'
- Become more aware about what is really happening globally behind the scenes
- Watch films like 'Thrive' at www.thrivemovement.com

I expect you are already doing several of these already and some of them are really quite simple and easy to implement into our lives. What else can you think of? If everyone, or nearly everyone, in the world were to do just 2 or 3 items on the two lists above, then what a difference that would make to the power of Light consciousness and the vibration of our current global consciousness.

What else can you think of? I hope you have been sparked into new ideas!

I really do hope that you can now see that we all have the power to make a difference in so many more ways than we thought possible. Just choosing Pure Light Consciousness or sending Love, Light and Peace to the world every day is making a really big difference to the energy of the world, and reducing the dominant dark power that is controlling us.

The shift from dark to Light and from war to peace depends on the majority using their united intentions and energy to out power dark energy.

Remember that dark has no natural source of energy so the more we use our power of free choice to disconnect from dark control and choose Light, the harder it will be for dark to have any power and energy of their own. When the majority in the world disconnect from fear and dark control, dark will end up in a struggle to just exist, as their energy supply runs out.

Awaken

The more we fill the world with Pure Love and Light energy, the more dark and evil will be purified or repelled, a bit like the wicked witch being dissolved by the bucket of water in the Wizard of Oz! Only this won't be a fairytale this will be real because energy is real, even though we can't see it. This is what the majority of people desire, and together we can create the world we desire by disconnecting from being dominated by evil. So much good is already being done. Companies are already working on ways to make electricity and power from natural resources, which will provide natural electricity for whole towns. Projects like replacing all windows with clear solar windows are being worked on; and having roads that create energy as cars drive over them! There are some really cool and incredible inventors out there doing some great stuff!

Not heard any of this, well that's no great surprise, as the main media channels are controlled by those wanting to control us; feeding us only the bad news to keep us under their control, and thinking we can't break free and create a better world, but we now know that we can and we ARE!

I do hope that you are now feeling awakened and inspired to do all you can to create peace! Please do share the information you have read in 'Awaken' with others, or even better recommend they buy a copy of 'Awaken' to read themselves!

Pure Love, Light & Peace

Awaken

Energy Work to Support You

Here is a summary of all the energy work I have given you in this book so you can refer back to it easily. You can find powerful audio energy work on my website at www.michellecarter.co.uk

I have also added some more energy work to help you 'Awaken'.

"I Consciously and Intentionally Use My Power of Free Choice to Choose Pure Love and Light"

Pure Love, Light & Peace

Quieten Your Mind

"I ask Divine Peace to fill and flow to your mind now, filling your mind with Divine Peace. Take a few deep breaths, close your eyes, and just feel all mind chatter float away, and feel peace and stillness. Allow this feeling of peace and stillness to stay with you as you connect to your feelings."

Disconnecting from fear

'I disconnect from this fear now'

'Pure Love and Light disconnects me from this fear now'

"Pure Source Energy / The Power of the Universe disconnects me from this fear now"

"Pure Love and Light disconnects me from all fear now and fills me with Pure Love and Light."

Awaken

Choosing Light

"I use my power of free choice to choose Pure Light Consciousness."

"I use the Power of the Universe, and my power of free choice to choose Pure Light Consciousness."

"I use the Power of the Universe, and my power of free choice to disconnect from the collective consciousness, and to choose Pure Light Consciousness."

"I use the Power of the Universe, the power of Pure love, the power of Pure Light and my power of free choice to choose Pure Light Consciousness."

"I use the Power of the Universe, the power of Pure love, the power of Pure Light, and my power of free choice to disconnect from the collective consciousness and to choose Pure Light Consciousness."

Pure Love, Light & Peace

Filling Statements

"Divine Peace fills and flows through your mind now. Allow Divine Peace to fill your mind, breathing out all anxiety, worry and stress, and filling with Divine Peace. As Divine Peace fills your mind, feel the stillness. Be still and enjoy the stillness."

"Pure Love fills your heart now. Allow Pure Love to fill and flow through your heart now, gently filling and expanding your heart energy. Feel your chest gently open and expand like a balloon being gently blown up, and allow the beautiful waves of Pure Love energy flow through your heart now."

"Pure Light fills your soul now. Allow Pure Light to fill and flow through your soul now, cleansing and purifying all connections to your soul guidance, so you feel clear, Pure guidance. Feel Pure Light fill and flow to your soul and ask for guidance on any issue you have."

Awaken

Clearing Releasing Energy

"I ask Pure Love & Light and the Power of the Universe to send all energies being released, cleared and disconnected direct to source, without feeling any releasing, processing or healing symptoms. Purifying all energies releasing and disconnecting now."

Disconnecting from Collective Consciousness

"Pure Love and Light and The Power of the Universe disconnects me from Collective Consciousness now, and sends all releasing and disconnecting energies direct to source; filling all space created with Pure Love and Light."

Pure Love, Light & Peace

Releasing Soul Barriers

"Pure Love & Light releases all blocks, barriers and energies preventing you from being connected to your soul, feeling discernment and your soul guidance. Sending all energies released direct to source, and filling with Divine Truth and Pure Light."

Releasing Statements

"I release all energies of . . . (sadness / anger) from me now"

"I ask Pure Love and Light to release all energies causing and creating . . . (sadness / anger) in me now, to send all energies released direct to source to be purified, and to fill me with Pure Love, Light, Peace & Joy to overflowing."

Moving Forwards

This book is about how we can 'Awaken', so I am not going to go into details about all I have learnt about Light and dark, and I'm not going to go into details about the human dark and evil that is going on in our world either. The reason for this is that my talents lie with energy work and I have actually learnt this information through other people and their research. I feel it is much better that you discover this direct from them, as information can become 'Chinese whispers' as it gets passed on, whereas you can get all the full facts and research direct from their websites, books and interviews, etc.

Pure Love, Light & Peace

My main reason for writing 'Awaken' was to use my energy channeling abilities to show you how to disconnect from fear, so you can find out whatever you wish to find out without feeling the fear that most people do feel when they discover this information. Also for you to know that there is no reason to feel fear when you understand the energy behind the scenes, and really understand the Power of the Universe and the Law of Attraction, and to know that the question isn't: -

Can we have peace on earth? –

but

How long is it going to take for enough people to awaken and choose peace?

When you fully believe that peace is attainable in your lifetime and that it is a question of numbers (people awakening to the information you have read), then you will be adding to the momentum of this shift to Light and Peace.

Please do read this book again because there is so much information in it, along with some powerful energy work, that it isn't possible to fully take it all in with just one reading. In fact, this book has been written with the intention that you can and will read it again and again, so you can have a deeper understanding of all the information in it each time

Awaken

you re-read it. Also the energy work has been added at the back of the book, so you can easily access it and read and work with it daily.

I have infused 'Awaken' with powerful Divine Energies, so you may feel these energies working as you read the book or hold it in your hands!

Some of the most awakening and enlightening information I have watched to find out more about what is happening in our physical world is the film – Thrive: What on Earth Will It Take? I expanded knowledge by watching interviews by David Icke, who is featured in the Thrive film.

There is much information available on the Internet when we start to look. Knowing the Truth whilst a bit scary at first is a freeing process. We cannot create change when we don't even know we are being controlled and are actually a victim of a system without even knowing it. Truth is empowering and the more people who choose to stand up for Truth, the quicker this will become our new reality.

If you wish to watch the film 'Thrive: What on Earth Will It Take?' or any other interviews, clips and videos then please do **disconnect from fear** before watching them. Doing this is preventing more fear being added to the global fear magnet!

Pure Love, Light & Peace

Any time you feel fear, or are in a moment of panic, (like when that huge black spider appears from nowhere!) - just say *'disconnecting from fear now'* and keep repeating it until you feel calmer, along with some *'Filling with Divine Peace'*, always a great one when you're feeling stressed or alarmed!

If you have enjoyed reading 'Awaken' then please do let me know, and leave some good reviews on Amazon and Goodreads.com to inspire others to also choose to create peace for us all.

You can find out more about me and my energy work on my website: www.michellecarter.co.uk including links to some interviews I have done with energy work, my blog, free information, samples, my audios and products and information about free live calls I do. Also when you sign up for my newsletter you will receive a free audio download!

I hope that we connect sometime in the future, and I would like to end this book by thanking you deeply with the whole of my heart and soul, for being the caring person that you are, for reading 'Awaken', for wishing to make a difference, and for taking action to: -

Create Heaven on Earth Now!

Thank you again for spending time with me reading

'Awaken'

Many Blessings
Michelle

www.ingramcontent.com/pod-product-compliance
Lightning Source LLC
Chambersburg PA
CBHW070625300426
44113CB00010B/1663